AF413256

ISBN 979-8-3302-7388-1

**This book was written for
Fiona Vandiver**

A special thanks to
Rubecca Wilson who has
been amazing support to
us in this journey.

A special thanks to the Families First program through the Missouri School For The Deaf, the First Steps program, and the Developmental Center of the Ozarks for all of the support that their staff and program have given us over the years

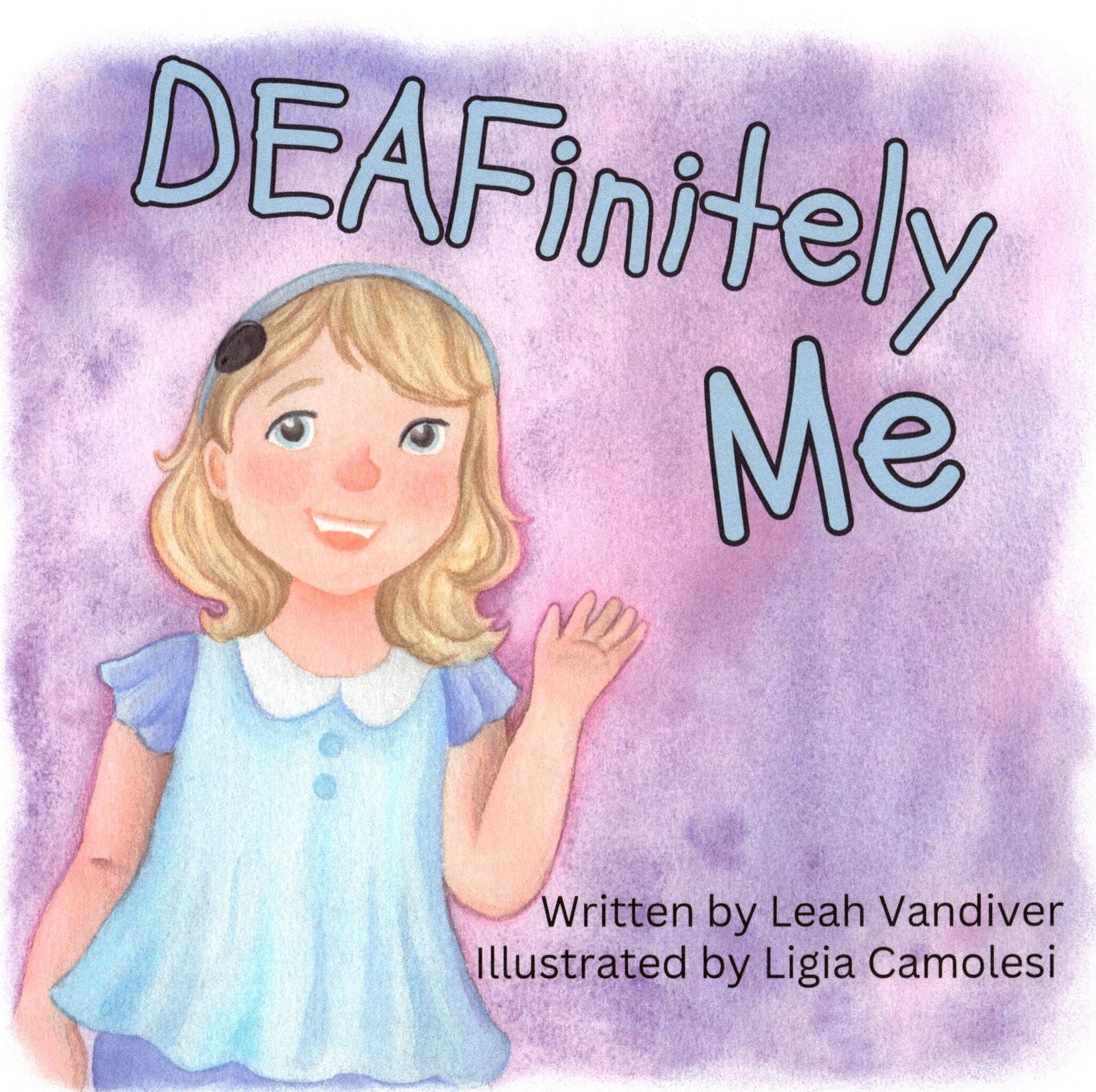


DEAFinitely Me
Written by Leah Vandiver
Illustrated by Ligia Camolesi

My name is Fiona. I am deaf in my right ear and hearing in my left ear.

I use a hearing aid that helps me everyday.

I am DEAFinitely
just me.

I love dressing up and my hearing aid makes me feel pretty.

I get to put pretty head bands on and add bows and stickers.

I am DEAFinitely
Pretty just the
way I am

I love to play outside with my brother.
My hearing aid helps me to have fun.

I am DEAFinitely good
at having fun.

My mom teaches me school at home.

My hearing aid helps me hear what she is teaching so that I can learn and explore.

# I am DEAFinitely smart.

My sisters love singing songs
and putting on shows
for the family.

My hearing aid helps me sing and dance along with them.

I am DEAFinitely a good singer and dancer.

Sometimes though I get tired of the extra hearing help and I need to take a break.

Although I can still hear some, we use ASL in our family to communicate and have quiet time.

I can DEAFinitely sign and talk

Everyone has something that makes them different from others and that's what makes us special and unique.

I am very loved and I am DEAFinitely and uniquely ME!

**ASL Resources:**

**National Institute on Deafness**

**National Association of the Deaf**

**Visual Language & Visual Learning**

**Deaf Library**

**ASL Browser**

handspeak.com

lifeprint.com

signingonline.com

startasl.com

# Great apps to learn ASL:

My Signing Time: lots of great baby and kid friendly videos to encourage and learn signing


Lingvano: an amazing app for adults and teens to use to learn ASL and go more in depth with the language.

# About the Author

Leah Vandiver is a mother to 6 beautiful children. As a mother of a child who wears a bone anchored hearing aid, she realized that children who need hearing help or ASL are not represented or understood as much and she hopes to change some of that with this book.